The Fit Mentor

How to Give People the Mentor they Need

Michael Heath

2012

The Fit Mentor

How to Give People the Mentor they Need

First Edition: June 2012

ISBN 978-1-9082931-5-2

Published by:

CGW Publishing
B 1502
PO Box 15113
Birmingham
B2 2NJ
United Kingdom

www.cgwpublishing.com

mail@cgwpublishing.com

This book is dedicated to my Mother

Christina Bridget Heath

The best of Mothers and the best of Mentors

Contents

A Meeting of Minds

Professor David Clutterbuck

There are many definitions and styles of Mentoring, so it's not surprising that research into what makes Mentoring relationships work comes up with very different answers. The factors that make two people "click" may be very different in a relationship based on sponsorship Mentoring (predominantly a North American phenomenon) to one based on developmental Mentoring (a European-originated approach now also widely used in North America). In the former, the relative power of Mentor and protégé are likely to play a significant role in the social exchange between them and hence in what each expects from the other. Ingratiation behaviours (Aryee REF) by the protégé and direct intervention by the Mentor in the protégé's career are also likely to be strong influencing factors in the perceived quality of the match. In the latter, the sense that both Mentor and Mentee have much to learn from each other has greater significance. Indeed, the absence of mutuality is likely to detract from perceived quality of relationship.

Relationship quality is partly to do with matching, partly to do with conduct and behaviours once the relationship is established. This book is about the first of these two elements and more specifically, about the process of formal matching. In informal Mentoring, people seek out or find Mentors or Mentees independently of an organization or programme. The Mentoring relationship may emerge out of other relationships in an organization or profession (for example, being part of a project team, or meeting at events run by a professional association. In formal Mentoring, there is some form of intervention to bring potential Mentors and Mentees together; however, the degree of formality may also vary considerably, from providing a database, in which Mentors and Mentees can self-match, to matching managed or controlled by a programme coordinator or other official. Irrespective of how the match is arranged, however, it is possible at a minimum to establish consistent good practice about how the process happens at its best.

In an unpublished study almost twenty years ago, I interviewed experienced Mentoring programme managers about how they decided who to match with whom. When they made good decisions (ones where both Mentors and Mentees felt well-matched) the programme managers' accounts revealed two consistent themes. One was that they looked at the potential for rapport; would the two people be able to get along with each other? The other was the potential for learning; was there enough difference in experience and perspective to create significant mutual learning? In most cases, this judgement was based on an instinctive understanding of the participants.

A limiting factor of this brief study was that the programmes represented almost all involved small numbers of participants, rarely more than 50 people, most of whom were known to the programme managers, to at least some degree. For those they didn't know so well, the programme managers typically sought the advice of other HR colleagues. Such personalized, intimate knowledge of participants isn't always practical with large numbers, so increasing attention has been directed in recent years to identifying ways to match participants, who aren't personally known to the programme managers.

Some of the key issues that organizations have had to consider in this context include:

What factors to take into account? In terms of establishing rapport, early studies indicated that personality was not a valid matching criterion (REF Alleman). Like any other kind of intimate partnership, Mentoring can work equally well when the two persons are similar in personality or different. Indeed, the difference can be a driver of the relationship and a key source of learning. Having a sense of shared values appears to have much greater validity (REF Hale). Recent experiments by Norway's Statoil (through the Swiss consultancy Mentorable) have partially validated Reiss Motivational Profiling (RMP) as a practical tool for assessing compatibility. (RMP looks at people's most powerful personal values.) Some of my own current research suggests that others factors may include geographical location (travelling to meet may be a good thing, because it builds in thinking time before and after!), learning maturity (compatibility of how people learn) and cultural awareness or openness.

Self-matching v "shot-gun marriages"

Many on-line Mentoring systems aim to reduce the burden on programme staff by enabling Mentees to select their own Mentors. Experience suggests that this works better with sponsorship Mentoring than developmental. Moreover, a good deal of support is needed to help participants make good choices. Left to their own devices, Mentees are likely to seek Mentors, who are too similar to themselves (limiting the learning potential). They are also less likely to look at alternatives outside their own career discipline or organizational silo. On the other hand, forced matches also don't have a particularly good track record. From my own observation, it seems that good practice is for guided choice, supporting Mentees in thinking through what they need a Mentor for and what sort of person will give them both the challenge and the support they desire. Some of the most successful programmes have offered Mentees a choice of up to three Mentors, with information about each one. Mentees are encouraged to interview each potential Mentor, to ask for more advice in making a decision, if they want it, and then to report back to each of the Mentors explaining the reasons for their choice. Although this sounds scary, it is highly beneficial. It reinforces commitment to the chosen relationship, on the part of both Mentor and Mentee. And it raises the profile of the Mentee with the unselected Mentors, who often become additional, ad hoc, informal Mentors.

Who defines what a good match looks like? The core requirement is that a good match should deliver significant learning. But it can also be seen as one that supports organizational goals, such as retention, or achieving diversity objectives. Other factors, which may be relevant, include the quality of dialogue and the resultant quality of the Mentee's thinking about career and personal development issues. In my workshops with Mentors and Mentees, I frequently ask them to define what they are looking for in an ideal Mentoring relationship and what that would mean in terms of selecting and matching. This data is often very valuable in terms of programme design. In one case, in a programme in Asia-Pacific, the expectations of Mentors (mostly expatriates) and Mentees (Western educated local employees) about the role of the Mentor and the behaviours expected were almost diametrically opposed. Exploring the two sides of what was expected helped both to modify their view of a good match.

Face to face or virtual? The qualities needed for effective Mentoring face to face are not necessarily the same as those for e-Mentoring (REF Clutterbuck & Hussain, 2010). Placing greater emphasis on e-Mentoring expands the potential Mentor pool geographically, and allows for much greater flexibility and choice in matching, but may reduce the number of capable Mentors, because not everyone can Mentor well using virtual media.

Rematching

The International Standards for Mentoring Programmes in Employment (ISMPE) emphasize the importance of having a process to ensure that matches, which don't work well, can be dissolved in a timely and supportive manner, with the Mentee moving on to another Mentor. The more firmly based the original match was in criteria the Mentee had identified, the easier the rematch typically seems to be. The programme manager can help them re-examine and perhaps revise their criteria; or help them develop different perspectives on how to interpret those criteria in terms of the Mentor pool available.

In the phenomenon known as "Second Wave Mentoring" (in which organizations, having implemented a number of

Mentoring initiatives, are now attempting to capture their learning about good practice and use it to build more robust, sustainable programmes), effective matching has become a central theme.

If the match is right, if participants have appropriate initial training and on-going support, then Mentoring delivers consistently high returns on investment. I welcome this book as a valuable contribution to this consolidation of good practice.

© David Clutterbuck, April 2012

Introduction

Michael Heath

To Mentor another human being is a noble act that will leave a legacy of your wisdom and insight long after the relationship has ended

We all Mentor. There are occasions in all our lives when someone turns to us. Think about it. A child who turns to a parent. Your friend who phones for advice. A brother or sister who needs to talk. An employee who seeks out their manager. Someone in work, not necessarily a direct report, who wants to tap into the considerable skills and knowledge you've accumulated.

Call it coach, advisor, counsel or Mentor, it doesn't matter. They need to talk because they know you've done the journey. You've travelled that road; you know the wrong turnings, cul-de-sacs, crossroads and short cuts. They know you've got the map.

But people want different things. They don't always want someone to tell them what to do. Sometimes they need someone who'll just listen. And some people can be good at one but not the other.

A good Mentor, a fit Mentor, has the measure of the person who has turned to them and knows how to respond. They can choose the correct Mentoring role that will help the person most.

So getting the relationship where there is a perfect fit between Mentor and Mentee is crucial. You may have experienced first-hand the situation where the Mentor you had wasn't the Mentor you needed. If that's happened then you will have seen and felt for yourself the ineffectiveness of that relationship.

This book helps you to avoid that. Should somebody seek you out as a Mentor, I would strongly urge you to give the Mentee Questionnaire to them and ask them to complete it. Likewise, you should answer the Mentor Questionnaire and compare your profile with that of your new charge. How close is the fit between what they want and what you're prepared to give?

Yet there is so much more I want to offer you. I want to guide you through the Mentoring cycle. I also want to discuss the boundaries of a Mentoring relationship: what they are and why they matter. Most of all, let me talk you through your Mentoring profile and point out the skills which your particular type of Mentor demands.

If you're looking for an academic treatise then this isn't your book. But if you want an easy-to-read, informative book that quickly tells you the route to becoming a truly fit Mentor, then read on.

The Fit Mentor

"What happens is not as important as how you react to what happens."

Thaddeus Golas

When a programme of Mentoring is thoughtfully prepared and implemented, the results are visible in those being Mentored almost from day one

Mentoring is increasingly seen as a great way of getting talented people to make a bigger impact, more quickly, within any organisation. When a programme of Mentoring is thoughtfully prepared and implemented, the results are visible in those being Mentored almost from day one.

But what about when the opposite happens? When a talented person is assigned a Mentor who is not suitable for their needs, skills or situation?

That is why this book is called 'The Fit Mentor'. A fit Mentor is someone who has been carefully selected to bring out the full potential of their charge. One-size Mentoring does not fit all. Research carried out in preparation for this book showed the following quite clearly; that people who desired a Mentor often had very clear ideas of who that person might be, the skills they would need and the style they would have to employ.

"But", I can hear you ask, "Sometimes we should get the Mentor we need, not the Mentor we want." Up to a point, yes. But unless there is real confidence in the Mentor from the outset then the relationship may not even get to the second meeting. Mentees I spoke to were very clear about this: they prefer someone who fits their particular need and resent having someone imposed from above.

To help you and your organisation achieve this Mentoring 'Nirvana' I have appended questionnaires that will help you to make a match in Mentoring Heaven. One questionnaire is for the potential Mentor, the other for the person they will be Mentoring. Both questionnaires will indicate the preferred styles of:

○ The type of Mentor the Mentee believes they will benefit most from

○ The type of Mentor a potential Mentor feels they are prepared to be

In the following pages I have set out what it takes to be a 'Fit' Mentor. Much of the material on which I have drawn comes from the testimonies of many people recounting successful Mentoring relationships that left them with life-long learning and benefits.

What is Mentoring?

"Don't just do it, stand there."

David Williams

Modern Mentoring is based on the notion of the 'wise and trusted counsellor'

Mentoring is hard to define as a discrete activity but all good Mentoring has personal and professional benefit to Mentees and Mentors

Mentoring helps individuals make a more speedy and effective contribution to the organisation

Mentoring enables individuals to make an effective contribution much earlier

A Mentor is whoever the Mentee perceives as being beneficial and desirable for them at that stage in their personal and professional development

What Does the Word 'Mentor' Mean?

We take the word from the Greek character Mentor, to whom Odysseus entrusted the care and education of his son, Telemachus. However, the word has been appropriated during the last century to mean 'a wise and trusted counsellor' and is a much-used concept in both business and academic life. Mentor is an appropriate name for such a person because it probably meant "adviser" in Greek and comes from the Indo-European root 'men-' meaning "to think".

What we should call the person being Mentored is much more problematic. For the sake of convenience I will use the word 'Mentee'. An ugly word but at least it will serve the purpose for the rest of this book.

What Do Mentors Do?

Our research indicated that the word 'Mentoring' covers a wide range of activities. Some people talked of Mentoring as being the process whereby you help someone settle into an organisation. Others spoke of specific, expert advice related to an individual's daily responsibilities. There were also many who felt it was someone who acted as a 'confidant', using coaching techniques to help the Mentee think for themselves or consider wider issues.

What background or experience should the Mentor come from? Some felt that it could be a colleague from the same team; it might be your manager or perhaps their manager; it might even be someone totally unconnected with what you do for a living.

And yet there was one thread that would be true of all Mentors; that they play a vital part in the Mentee's development; perhaps the acquisition of a new piece of knowledge or skill; it might even be a profound shift in the mindset of the Mentee. Whatever the benefit, the Mentor had a key role to play.

But does this answer the question? No, in fact, it raises more questions than ever! But it leads us to a conclusion which respects all of the different views we met with during the research:

A Mentor is whoever the Mentee perceives as being beneficial and desirable for them at that stage in their personal and professional development

Why Mentor?

Individuals benefit from other more experienced, more expert, more capable people to help them. Whether it be someone who acts as a 'Buddy' for a recent arrival, or someone who a Mentee uses as a 'sounding board' for giving vent to new concepts, doubts and scarcely articulated ideas, the Mentee has much to gain from the relationship.

All organisations need individuals to contribute quickly and effectively; Mentoring helps with that aim. It supports, listens, guides and enables. It challenges, encourages and inspires. Many Mentees, many years on, can easily recall those who played a significant role in their personal development and the value they received from the relationship then, and probably still benefit from today.

Without doubt, a Mentored individual progresses much more quickly than an individual who has no Mentor. They spend less time getting sidetracked by tangential or marginal issues (or people) and contribute much earlier to their work objectives.

How Will the Mentor Benefit?

There's great value to be had for the Mentor as well. The open-minded learn from working closely with someone who thinks differently, tackles issues differently, or has new ideas, new approaches. Before their eyes they may see a steady growth in stature, thinking and self-confidence and learn not only about the nature of an individual within their working environment, but also about the nature of human beings themselves.

Mentoring Relationships

"A lot of people have gone further than they thought they could because someone else thought they could."

Anonymous

There are four key participants in Mentoring

There should be close liaison maintained between the manager and Mentor

Introduction of new people into the Mentoring relationship must be communicated to all participants

What Are The Relationships In The Mentoring Process?

Many view the Mentoring relationship as only being between the Mentor and Mentee. However, there are four key participants in the Mentoring process:

1. Manager: this could be the Mentee's own manager or a manager drawn from another department, for example an advisor within HR

2. Employee: the individual being Mentored (the Mentee)

3. Mentor(s): Successful Mentoring might involve more than one Mentor

4. Other Contacts: relationships which are established by either the Manager, Mentee or Mentor as a result of the Mentoring process

Of course, all participants in the process would benefit from some degree of liaison with each other; these key relationships are illustrated below.

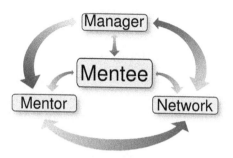

The Need for Communication Between Manager and Mentor

An individual is usually invited to be a Mentor by either the Mentee or their Manager; once the Mentor has agreed to fulfil the role it is vital all parties agree the basis of the Mentoring relationships. For example, the manager might value the Mentor's professional reputation in a particular area, or they may want the Mentor to develop the wider thinking of the Mentee. Both examples would require the Mentor to carry out the task in subtly different ways.

The regularity of liaison between the Manager and Mentor depends on how the Manager might view the relationship. Some Managers might welcome a close relationship with the Mentor; other Managers might only want occasional feedback. Managers may even derive their feedback about the success of the Mentoring experience from the Mentee themselves.

Whichever feedback mechanism the Manager chooses, by establishing and maintaining an appropriate link with the Mentee's Manager the Mentor will ensure that they have every opportunity to be an effective resource to the Mentee.

Introducing Other Contacts

There may well be occasions when the Mentor decides that a particular need lies outside her or his own abilities. When this occurs, the natural progression is for the Mentor and Mentee to establish if there is another individual who may meet this particular need and who would be willing to help. Where this happens it is vital that all participants be made aware about the inclusion of another party, whether they be an additional Mentor or a much more short-term solution.

The Mentoring Cycle

*"We make a living by what we get, we make a
life by what we give."*

Winston Churchill

Mentors should be identified by consensus between both manager and Mentee

Managers, Mentors and Mentees should be clear about what they want from the relationship and be able to articulate this and reach agreement

Aims and objectives give the relationship focus and provide a measure against which the success of the relationship can be assessed

Evaluation of the Mentoring relationship provides excellent feedback and insight to all parties

A Step-By-Step Approach to the Mentoring Cycle

The following cycle can provide a useful starting point for those Mentors and Mentees setting out on such a relationship for the first time.

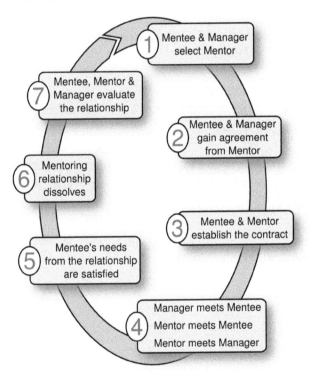

1. Mentee and Manager select Mentor

Some Mentees have pointed out that they would prefer to find their own Mentor, some even talking of 'gravitating' towards their eventual Mentor.

While the serendipitous approach of the latter can have benefits, there is still a strong chance that the Mentee might end up finding someone they want, but not necessarily someone they need.

In 'Mentoring Relationships', we discussed the fact that: "An individual is usually invited to be a Mentor by either the Mentee or their Manager; once the Mentor has agreed to fulfil the role it is vital all parties agree the basis of the Mentoring relationships."

Of course there might be some validity for a Manager to select a Mentor independently of the Mentee, but my recommendation would be that the decision is a consensual one arrived at after a thorough examination of what the benefits would be for that Mentee.

Imposing a Mentor on the potential Mentee can be negatively perceived; after all, a particular individual may do very well without any Mentoring whatsoever.

Another factor is that mismatches can occur, either in developmental needs or simply with a clash of personalities.

However, a good Mentoring match has many positive outcomes for all parties: but the final choice must always rest with the Mentee, and the relationship can then be enthusiastically entered into on all sides.

My research strongly identified that the more ownership the Mentee has with their choice, the more positively they enter into the relationship.

2. Mentee and Manager gain agreement from Mentor

Mentors are often very busy people. They are also, often, generous people, both with their time and their resources. It is therefore imperative that they are approached with these caveats in mind.

When approaching a potential Mentor, Managers or Mentees need to bring a clear brief of what they want the relationship to achieve.

Such a brief might comprise:

- A brief outline of the Mentee: their career and aspirations
- What the Mentoring relationship needs to achieve
- How this aim relates to their broader development
- Specific objectives that will indicate that the relationship is successful
- The amount of time likely to fulfil the role
- The anticipated demands on time the relationship might entail
- The likely media and venue for the relationship to take place
- The degree of confidentiality that should be established
- Why the potential Mentor has been chosen
- What value they believe the Mentor might bring to the relationship
- The particular role they would like the potential Mentor to play
- The process of review and feedback

3. Mentor and Mentee establish the contract

Boundaries of the Relationship

This subject is covered in full in the 'The Boundaries of Mentoring' section.

Outcomes and Objectives

A Mentoring relationship must have a purpose, otherwise it will soon lose its direction and impetus and eventually become devalued by all parties. Outcomes and objectives help avoid this by fixing definite targets or aims that both parties want the relationship to move towards.

In some Mentoring relationships these are easy to establish; for instance, it might be that the Mentee wants to prepare a budget application for a substantial project. Such an outcome will be easy to measure when the money is made available – or not!

Other aims may be more nebulous. Perhaps the Mentee wants to deepen their thinking in a particular discipline, or needs a 'sounding board' with whom they can share issues such as role or organisational tensions.

Whatever the aim, it should be clearly articulated and agreed by the Mentor, Mentee, Manager and any other contacts that might temporarily enter the relationship.

Some aims can be underpinned by specific objectives, which bring the needs of the Mentee into sharper focus.

Returning to our earlier example of someone applying for budget for their project, the stated aim can be supported by specific objectives that become milestones along the Mentoring journey. These milestones might be:

○ The development of a specific budget

○ The successful submission of their request

○ Identifying, through a network, the outcomes of the project which will be more positively considered

○ Identifying previous project applications and why they were successful.

All of the above objectives can be clarified at the earliest opportunity by the Mentor and Mentee, and give real direction to subsequent meetings.

4a. Mentor and Mentee meet

Once all of the earlier stages have been carried out, the way is open for the Mentoring process to move towards the actual meeting of Mentor and Mentee. On rare occasions, it may be possible for this meeting to take place over the telephone or through some other form of suitable media. Subsequent interactions do not necessarily demand a meeting, and both parties may be content with less formal communication.

However, if a more formal meeting is chosen, then this should be conducted using the general advice on environment and other practicalities found in the section 'Practical Considerations when Mentoring'.

4b. Manager and Mentee meet

Many Mentoring situations, especially those co-ordinated with the involvement of the employee's manager, will often involve some feedback being given. Depending on the original agreement about the level of confidentiality, these meetings will have different degrees of depth and range: some will be brief assurances as to whether or not the Mentoring relationship is proving worthwhile, whilst others will explore the success of the relationship in some detail.

4c. Manager and Mentor meet

Some Mentoring relationships have been set up to provide feedback to the manager on the Mentee's progress. For instance, the employee may be new and the manager has assigned the Mentor to give him or her feedback about their capability over the employee's first weeks or months of employment.

Usually, where this is the case, this feedback loop is communicated to the Mentee so that they understand the limited confidentiality that the relationship can accommodate. Not to tell the Mentee that this is the case could have a serious effect on all relationships within the arrangement and even extend to other Mentoring relationships within the organisation.

Some characterise these positive Mentoring relationships as 'HOT': honest, open and trusting.

5. Mentee's needs from the relationship are satisfied

Some Mentoring relationships with highly defined objectives may have a relatively short life, especially when those objectives are related to a specific area of knowledge or skill (think of our Research budget application example given earlier). There will also be Mentoring relationships that will be open-ended, with, perhaps, the focus on counselling or coaching over a much longer time frame.

The fact that a relationship has met the needs of the Mentee should be identifiable by the satisfaction of the original aim and objectives agreed at the first meeting.

Of course, some relationships exhaust these and continue because new objectives develop and eventually supersede those which were first agreed. This would need to be recognised and agreed by all parties and have the broad commitment of the same to the continuation of the Mentoring relationship under an altered remit. Should this happen, then certain individuals will ask for the original Mentoring contract to be re-written to reflect this.

6. Mentoring relationship dissolves

Once it has been recognised by all parties that the relationship has run its course, there will come a time for a formal ending of the Mentoring process.

On many occasions the Mentor recognises that their contribution has maybe become exhausted and that the Mentee needs to explore further development with other Mentors. Equally, this fact may be recognised by the Mentee and it is they who initiate the eventual cessation of the relationship. Unfortunately some relationships dissolve because of an inherent mismatch between the Mentor and Mentee, and one or other (or both!) of the parties recognises that the resulting value of the arrangement is being impaired.

Mentoring is not a 'one-off' event in a person's life, but can take place as part of a series of Mentoring relationships or even in parallel with other Mentoring experiences.

7. Mentee, Mentor and Manager evaluate the relationship

There is a world of difference between Mentoring being a 'general chat' and a tool which gives individuals real encouragement and value. Sometimes a 'general chat' might indeed be what is called for; nevertheless, as much as Mentoring can be demanding on people's time, it is important to make sure that the whole exercise is appropriate and beneficial.

Obviously evaluation is not something that should take place only at the end. There will be many informal, and perhaps formal, evaluations that take place over the lifetime of the relationship, but it is certainly the time when all of those involved can articulate their degree of satisfaction with the whole exercise and try to assess it's worth and contribution.

Evaluation is at its most effective when centred on the specific objectives that framed the Mentoring need.

Questions to explore might include:

○ Were the objectives of the Mentoring relationship achieved?

○ To what extent were they achieved?

○ Were they the right objectives agreed upon at the outset?

○ What learning has taken place as a result of the Mentoring relationship?

The Mentor and Mentee might also want to explore their own contribution to the relationship, and even assess the contribution of each other.

Whether such evaluation is formalised or not is down to the individuals in the Mentoring relationship, but even informal evaluation will yield much benefit to all and help each individual when they progress to other Mentoring experiences in whichever capacity: manager, Mentee or Mentor.

The Boundaries of Mentoring

> *"Correction does much, but encouragement more; encouragement after censure is as the sun after a shower."*
>
> *Goethe*

Successful Mentoring relationships establish clear boundaries

There are three boundary areas to agree: time, place or medium, confidentiality or expertise

A Mentoring Contract formalizes these boundaries and should also cover the aim and objectives of the relationship

Why Have Boundaries?

If a Mentoring relationship is to be a fulfilling one for all parties, then it is vital that clear and unambiguous boundaries are established at the outset. These boundaries ensure that the 'rules of Mentoring engagement' are agreed and honoured by those involved. A failure to agree these boundaries may lead to ambiguity or confusion and, if not addressed, might result in the eventual breakdown of the Mentoring experience.

What Boundaries Should Be Agreed?

At the initial meeting, it is vital to define three essential boundary areas:

1. Time Boundaries

2. Place and Media Boundaries

3. Confidentiality and Expertise Boundaries

Time Boundaries

Some Mentoring relationships can be more time-consuming than others; some are initially demanding on time but eventually become less so. Whatever the situation, the Mentor and Mentee must give some considerable thought to:

○ The amount of time they envisage will be demanded of the relationship

○ The amount of time they have available to commit to the relationship

○ The degree of 'formality' of the relationship itself

Some Mentoring relationships are extremely informal, with the Mentee seeking out their Mentor only on certain occasions. Other relationships demand a much more formal approach that often results in a regular time being set aside for the Mentoring session.

Both the Mentor and Mentee need to carefully articulate their understanding of the impression to ensure that both parties have similar anticipation of what will be demanded. With this agreed, a reasonable time for meetings can then be established.

Place and Media Boundaries

Different Mentoring relationships demand different environments. Some Mentoring meetings always take place away from the Mentee's normal place of work; doing this is sometimes felt to aid original thinking or help relax both Mentor and Mentee in more convivial surroundings.

Other Mentoring meetings take place in offices or areas of work. Again, there may well be good reasons for this: perhaps important equipment is near at hand, or access may be needed to key texts or materials during the meeting. There are some Mentoring relationships that use different media such as telephone, video-conferencing or email.

As with time, some aforethought on the part of both parties will soon indicate the 'place' which will be deemed the most suitable for the meetings. Again, once both parties have established where this should be, then there should be no subsequent ill feeling or disagreement about the Mentoring venue or media chosen.

One final thought: some Mentors have been known to suggest relaxed areas such as bars to conduct the Mentoring session. A general 'rule of thumb' for Mentoring is that the area should be one without distraction and interruption. Venues such as bars do not always meet such criteria and may even, in rare cases, work against the success of the meeting itself.

Confidentiality and Expertise Boundaries

My research within both Mentor and Mentee groups clearly showed that there were very different expectations of the Mentoring relationship. Some viewed it as 'Guidance' and 'Subject expertise' whilst others saw it as touching upon much deeper issues such as personal experiences and problems.

The potential for mismatch can be avoided only by the Mentor and Mentee being absolutely clear about how wide they want the boundary to be. Some will see it purely as a forum to improve personal knowledge and understanding. Others will want to explore issues that are wider, perhaps directed towards personal learning and growth.

Again this will need to be clarified and agreed by all parties. Confidentiality can sometimes be impossible because of the

Mentor's responsibilities to an organisation. If this is the case then this should be clearly communicated at the outset. Also, some Mentors do not feel that they have the necessary skills to handle personal issues, and may well feel uncomfortable when asked to become involved in such conversations.

Therefore, the Mentor must accurately set out the degree to which the conversation can remain confidential. Likewise, the Mentee must say what their understanding of the boundary of confidentiality is so that they're confident where such limits have been set.

Expertise boundaries are usually established before the Mentoring meeting. If the Mentor's manager has set up the relationship, then it is to be hoped that they have given serious thought to the reason why they have chosen a certain individual to Mentor their employee. Whatever the reason, the boundary of expertise, like time, place and confidentiality, must be specified and communicated before the relationship progresses.

The Mentoring Contract

The boundaries of a Mentoring relationship can be set out in a written contract, the formality of which will depend on the situation. This can be a useful document that not only communicates the agreed boundaries to the Mentor and Mentee, but also to the Mentee's manager so that they understand the basis of the relationship.

Such a contract might include:

1. The anticipated outcomes of the Mentoring relationship

This will be an overall aim for the Mentoring relationship. What do all parties want the purpose of the relationship to be?

2. Specific objectives

By agreeing specific objectives, the Mentee can log their progression to ensure that their needs and wants from the relationship are being covered. This can also be linked into their personal development plan.

3. Agreed boundaries for the Mentoring relationship

To cover boundaries of time, place, medium, confidentiality and expertise.

Who Drives The Relationship?

"Mentoring is a brain to pick, an ear to listen,
and a push in the right direction."

John Crosby

_____

There is no set format to how and when Mentoring should take place

The needs of the Mentee should dictate to what extent the meetings are formally or informally arranged

Whose Responsibility is it to Make it happen?

The degree to which one person or other takes responsibility for making sure that full advantage is taken of the relationship depends on the nature of the relationship itself. Some Mentees will want to speak with their Mentor when they hit a 'brick wall' or just need someone to bounce ideas off. Another Mentee may only feel in need of their Mentor when there is a something fairly minor which they need explaining.

I am reluctant to 'lay down the law' on the issue as successful Mentoring partnerships very often find their own way. Some Mentoring relationships may agree at the outset, and even declare in the Mentoring contract, that both will seek each other out when they feel it would be good to do so.

Some Mentors spoke of how the relationship with their Mentee was on a very informal 'ad hoc' basis; if they hadn't heard from their Mentee for some time, then they would casually seek them out to see how things were going.

Other relationships, where particular value is placed on a regular session, tend to have equal energies from both sides keeping the momentum of the meetings going.

What is important, however, is that the relationship's activities and impetus are centred on the needs of the Mentee. A skilled Mentor may drive much of the relationship early on (perhaps they are in a more senior position to the Mentee) but they may well pass responsibility gradually over to the Mentee as their confidence climbs during the relationship.

Again, at the risk of making the point ad nauseam, this is why setting the time boundary at the outset is so vital.

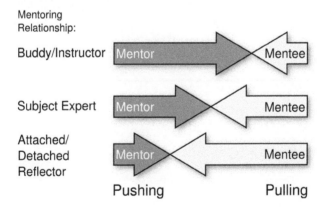

Mentoring Relationship:

Buddy/Instructor — Mentor → Mentee

Subject Expert — Mentor → Mentee

Attached/ Detached Reflector — Mentor → Mentee

Pushing   Pulling

Understanding Rapport

"One of the most valuable things we can do to heal one another is listen to each other's stories."

Rebecca Falls

Rapport is a harmony that lies between two people; it is much more than merely 'getting on' with someone

We can easily build rapport by using 'The Rapport Cycle'

There are a number of body language factors which help stimulate and maintain strong rapport

What is Rapport?

A point often made when covering the subject of Mentoring is the need to 'build rapport'. But what exactly is rapport and what should we be doing to encourage it?

Definitions of rapport are many and varied, my personal preference being to view it as the strengthening of a relationship through trust and a mutual affinity. Why is rapport so important in Mentoring? Well, a relaxed Mentee who feels comfortable with their Mentor is going to enjoy the session so much more, rapport contributing to that sense of ease.

Many people just view rapport as 'getting on together'. But real rapport is much more than that: it is a sense that both individuals feel a real empathy for each other; they enjoy a familiarity and warmth that marks out the relationship in a very different way.

Why Should I Create Rapport?

Building rapport is particularly essential at the beginning of the first session; it helps create a pleasant atmosphere as both Mentor and Mentee 'sound out' each other. Rather than driving straight into the session itself, it enables both parties to gradually ease into the substance of the Mentoring session by degrees.

Once this sense of ease has been established, the Mentee will feel that they are talking with someone who is more attuned to their situation and will 'open up' all the more because of the trust that is now present.

There are Mentoring relationships where such rapport isn't apparent yet which have value in spite of that. But the relationships which have rapport, warmth and genuine fellow-feeling are often more stimulating and honest, reflecting the comfort both parties feel in each other's company.

How do I Create rapport?

One simple method of building rapport is to use 'The Rapport Cycle':

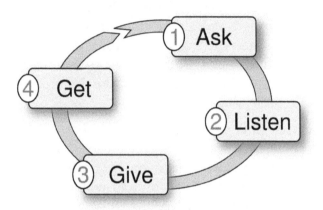

Ask

At the outset of your first Mentoring meeting you might ask a general question which is totally unrelated to the Mentoring topics you will be discussing. It may be the car the person's driving, the University they went to or the book they might be carrying.

Listen

Once you've asked your question you will listen intently to what they say and show that you're listening by using the appropriate body language and gestures.

The Fit Mentor

Give

Once they've finished speaking you have the chance to respond with conversation that is directly and closely linked to what they've just told you. What's most important here is to tell them something about yourself as you do so, so that they see you as an open person who is comfortable revealing personal details, hopefully stimulating a similar degree of candour in the Mentee. It may be wise to reveal something that is within your professional life in order to safeguard your boundaries.

Get

Now, hopefully, they will also respond and help cement that common area of conversation that you've both just created. Now the cycle can begin again.

Of course you may look at the above and exclaim "But isn't this obvious?" Well, to some, it is. But, occasionally, Mentees I spoke to berated their Mentors as 'distant' or 'aloof'. It would appear that their Mentors viewed rapport as a 'foreign country'! You have probably experienced for yourself the company of an individual who seemed 'difficult to get to know'. Would you want to open up to that person?

Body Language and Rapport

There are many who subscribe to the view that mirroring the posture and voice of the Mentee will stimulate a greater degree of rapport. Others will argue that such 'aping' of another person may be misinterpreted as patronising or 'playing games' with the Mentee.

It's probably best to put both arguments aside and think carefully about how you can naturally position yourself so as to demonstrate your genuine interest in the Mentee.

Good eye contact is essential and, probably more than any other gesture, conveys interest and attentiveness. However, merely resting your eyes on the Mentee's face is not going to be enough. If your eyes are expressionless then you may appear bored to the Mentee or they may think your mind has wandered onto much more interesting subjects!

Leaning forward or sitting upright again shows that you're engaged with the Mentee. Some Mentors adopt the 'guru' pose of leaning back, elbows on the arm of their chair with their fingers touching just in front of their face. This may look 'intellectual' to some but is often viewed as a little patronising by others, even superior.

When training new Mentors I always run the 'CEO test' with people. I would ask, "How would you sit and what eye contact would you use if you were seated around a boardroom table with your CEO?" Overwhelmingly, most state that they would sit upright and show the excellent eye contact referred to above. My approach is to then reply, "Then why conduct yourself in any other way when Mentoring? Do they not deserve the same basic expression of esteem for a human being as your CEO?"

Expressive facial responses are key to conveying that you're not only listening, but reacting as a human being, to the conversation of your Mentee. We have all experienced that awful moment when a punch line to a joke is met with an embarrassing silence by our audience. Well, the same happens when we talk about something deeply important to us only to see an emotionless 'mask' looking straight back at us.

A lack of physical expressiveness to a Mentee can suddenly make them withdraw and they may be much less inclined to open up in later sessions.

Not interrupting the Mentee is a skill that is all about sensing the moment to speak and when to let the Mentee do the talking. It's about providing a 'silent space' where the Mentee feels comfortable wrestling with their thoughts and emotions as they try to grapple with a difficult matter.

There's no denying that not speaking is an art; it takes a combination of sensitivity and insight to know when to add your own thoughts as a Mentor and when to keep quiet.

Those Mentors with a tendency to play the 'Guru' in their sessions will never be able to hold back; they will see silences as the chance to add a 'business insight' or recount a well-worn anecdote dusted off from their personal business memoirs. Good Mentors will realise that the session is for the primary benefit of the Mentee and will withhold their own counsel to allow the Mentee time to think things through.

Moderating your voice to that of the Mentee can really help build the levels of rapport in a session. If you are faced with a quiet, reflective Mentee, then they will baulk at the 'bulldozer' who speaks quickly and decisively.

Conversely, a gregarious, outgoing Mentee may find their communication strangely negated by a withdrawn and quiet disposition in their Mentor.

One doesn't have to markedly change one's communication style when Mentoring, but we do have an obligation to express ourselves in way that reflects the dominant style of communication of our Mentee.

Reflective Practice in Mentoring

"The greatest good you can do for another is not just to share your riches but to reveal to him his own."

Benjamin Disraeli

Mentors should avoid assuming a 'Guru' role with Mentees

Reflective Practice allows the Mentee to stand back from their activities and to critically assess their work

A Mentor uses the acronym 'DATA' to stimulate Reflective Practice: Describe, Analyse, Theorise and Act

Avoiding the 'Guru' Approach to Mentoring

Ex-racing driver, John Whitmore, in his popular book 'Coaching for Performance' believed that: "To ask is to acknowledge a person's intelligence; to tell is to deny it." The need for a sound understanding of questioning and listening skills goes deeper than that even inferred by Whitmore; helping someone reflect and explore issues, decisions and consequences for themselves has much greater impact than if the Mentor merely acted as a 'Guru' for the Mentee: supplying all of the answers without any input from the Mentee at all.

One aim in many Mentoring sessions is to stimulate the Mentee to seek out their own answers to the situations they bring to the meeting. Yes, we can help with alternatives and even solutions if need be, but the primary role of the Mentor is to help the Mentee to grow and develop. Merely giving the Mentee the answers prevents this vital learning process from occurring.

What is Reflective Practice?

It could best be described as a method that links thought and action with reflection. It is about engaging the Mentee to think about and critically analyse their actions with the overall aim of improving their attitude, skills and understanding in the workplace.

It allows the Mentee to stand back from their activities and to explore consequences and outcomes of their work; good Mentors encourage the Mentee to look critically at their work and to analyse why they do the things they do in the way that they do.

One thinker on Reflective Practice, R B Kottkamp (1990), used the terms "offline" and "online" to distinguish between reflection-on-action and reflection-in-action. The role of the Mentor is completely with encouraging the former: 'reflection-on-action'.

By helping the Mentee analyse their actions, new conclusions are reached which, hopefully, result in more successful working practices.

The reflective process is vital, as the Mentee must understand how they have arrived at this new place. The route that they take is equally as important as the answer that they arrive at because, on the journey, they may well have discovered new skills that can be applied to other situations.

This method of analysis is especially important to those Mentees whose intention is not consistent with their action. That is, what they say they will do professionally, and what they then go on to do, are not the same. The Mentor must help the Mentee uncover the reasons why they are behaving in an inconsistent manner so that they can align their behaviour with their intent.

How Do We Encourage Reflective Practice?

Because of the nature of Reflective Practice, the Mentor has to be prepared to spend considerable time in helping the Mentee work through issues that they are faced with.

Here is a list of questions (based on the work of Robert A Roth, 1989) which can be used to stimulate the necessary critical thinking on behalf of the Mentee.

- Questioning what, why, and how one does things and asking what, why, and how others do things
- Seeking alternatives
- Keeping an open mind
- Comparing and contrasting
- Seeking the framework, theoretical basis, or underlying rationale
- Viewing from various perspectives
- Asking "what if...?"
- Asking for others' ideas and viewpoints
- Using prescriptive models only when adapted to the situation
- Considering consequences
- Hypothesizing
- Synthesizing and testing
- Seeking, identifying, and resolving problems

Some Mentors need a defined structure or process within which these questions can sit, and one of the most commonly used is that of John M Peters, which he called DATA.

DATA

Describe — Analyse — Theorise — Act

Describe

The Mentee first identifies and describes something that they would like to change. They would then give the context in which this task or problem occurs, how they feel about it and the reason why they would like to change it.

Analyse

The second stage necessitates the Mentee analysing the situation they described and identifying why they have taken the current approach that has caused the outcome that now dissatisfies them. Through analysis they would hope to uncover their underlying beliefs and motives that have created this situation.

The Fit Mentor

Theorise

This stage sees the Mentee developing alternative approaches to the issue or problem that help them move away from their previous approach. Each theory is considered in some depth before the Mentee arrives at the most useful way to proceed.

Act

The Mentee will now try out this new theory and seek to ensure that there will be an aligned correspondence between their 'intent' and their eventual 'action'. The Mentor can help the Mentee at this point by asking them to cite potential 'road blocks' to their action, and thus avoid the sense of disappointment that might ensue.

Questioning and Listening Techniques

"The more you lose yourself in something bigger than yourself, the more energy you will have."

Norman Vincent Peale

Skilled Mentors' use four distinct types of questions: Open, Closed, Probing and Reflective

Open Questions, asked without inferring any judgement, stimulate the Mentee to 'open up' in their responses

Mentees respond best to 'Active Listeners', those that give full and direct attention to them

The Need for Skilled Questioning

Elsewhere we discussed how the success of Reflective Practice (See 'The use of Reflective Practice in Mentoring') depends upon the quality of questioning that is demonstrated by the Mentor; it is only through skilled questioning that a Mentee can effectively analyse, and apply critical thinking to, their activities.

The Four Different Types of Questions

There are four main types of questions that Mentors should use:

○ Open

○ Closed

○ Probing

○ Reflective

Good questioning skills allow you to focus the conversation, so that you and the Mentee keep to the point and the Mentoring session is more productive. Where possible you should try to ask questions that avoid judgement of the Mentee. Allow the Mentee, stimulated by your neutral questions, to pass judgement on their own actions.

Open Questions

These encourage the Mentee to talk openly and freely. They begin with the words 'who', 'what', 'why', 'where', 'when' and 'how'.

Examples:

- What approach did you have in mind?
- How would people have been affected by your decision?

Closed Questions

These should be used far less than open questions unless you are encouraging the Mentee to reach some form of conclusion or decision. They often begin with words such as 'Is', 'Can', 'If', 'Shall', 'Do', etc.

Examples:

- Did the presentation go as you planned?
- Is that the result you were looking for?
- Did you clarify with your colleagues exactly which action you felt was the most appropriate?

Probing Questions

Often used to allow the Mentee to consider and explore their feelings and actions at a deeper level. Often the response that you elicit may give the Mentee help with understanding an underlying motivation.

Examples:

○ You said that your colleagues might react badly to this. What were your reasons for thinking this?

○ When she'd asked you to contact her, what preparation had you made before you called her back?

○ What specific point in the conversation did you feel that you had lost control of the meeting?

Reflective Questions

These are used for summarising key areas of the conversation, to check the details gathered so far. They serve two purposes:

○ As a check that you've captured essential areas of information before you move onto other areas

○ To show the Mentee that you are taking what they say very seriously because you're summarising what you're hearing

Examples:

○ So up to now you hadn't thought such an approach necessary?

○ So once you had the problem clarified then he started to communicate more reasonably with you?

○ What you're really saying then is that you were caught out by the negative reaction to your initial suggestion?

Actively Listening to the Mentee

Just because you may be looking at the Mentee when they are speaking, doesn't necessarily mean that you are listening! To listen attentively to somebody means to develop the key skills that ensure that you understand all that is being said, and sometimes being skilful enough to understand what is not being said. There are three levels to listening as described by Dr Tony Alessandra:

○ Marginal

○ Evaluative

○ Active

Marginal Listening

Some people have the capacity to look interestedly at the Mentee when, in reality, their mind is very much elsewhere. Should your thoughts be taken up with a separate, and worrying, issue then you shouldn't really be Mentoring until this has been cleared from your mind. If the Mentee suspects that you are occupied mentally with something else, and are just going through the motions of listening, then any level of trust or confidence she or he may have might suffer.

Marginal Listeners usually demonstrate their listening state by:

○ Fixed eye contact with no movement of the eye at all

○ Fixed facial muscles

○ Failure to respond to key points with an appropriate response

○ Physical or verbal reactions which are not appropriate to the content of the Mentee's message

○ Any embarrassing silence that ensures once the Mentee has finished talking to allow the Mentor to respond

Evaluative Listening

Evaluative listeners are almost a 'halfway house' between the two extremes. They tend to absorb much of what the Mentee says but soon turn their mental attention to preparing a response rather than listening to the Mentee's message in its entirety. They may be better than the marginal listeners, but they are still prone to:

○ 'Jumping in' before the Mentee has finished their sentence

○ Displaying either a verbal (e.g. "Yes, yes, yes, but...") or non-verbal (e.g. a raised palm of the hand to stop the Mentee speaking) signal to allow them to interrupt

○ Missing a point made towards the latter half of the Mentee's contribution

○ Concluding too early the content of the Mentee's contribution and then framing a response based on what they've concluded

○ Finishing the Mentee's sentences

Active Listening

Active Listening demands more mental effort from the Mentor, requiring high levels of concentration to capture accurately all that is being said. To allow true Reflective Practice to take place, it is imperative that the Mentor builds a series of questions that allow the Mentee to logically explore a problem or issue. A person who is deficient in this skill reveals this through a failure to ask probing questions that are linked skilfully to one another. Active listeners:

○ Avoid interrupting the Mentee

○ Link their questions logically together based on the Mentee's line of thinking

○ Maintain good eye contact and body language

○ Fail to respond to petty distractions

○ Lean forward and use open hand gestures

○ Use non-verbal listening signals (Occasionally nodding their head, smiling at appropriate moments)

The Different Mentoring Styles

"The wise adapt themselves to circumstances,
as water moulds itself to the pitcher."

Chinese proverb

The skills of the Mentor must be carefully matched to the needs of the Mentee

There are four major Mentoring styles, each with a unique approach

Mentees can end up with the wrong Mentor for a variety of reasons, all of which can be avoided at the outset

Why is it Important to Recognise the Different Styles?

If one is to achieve a successful Mentoring relationship it is essential that a Mentor be assigned who matches the needs of the Mentee at that stage in their development. Mentors have strengths and weaknesses; the assigning of a Mentor who is unable to draw upon their strengths, due to the lack of consideration given to the pairing of Mentor to Mentee, can lead to a very dissatisfying experience for all involved.

My research found that, when people described what they believed Mentoring to be, the term came to represent very different things to different people. This gave rise to the concept of 'The Fit Mentor', one who is chosen because they fit the needs of the Mentee so well.

The following model is based on two characteristic needs of a Mentee:

○ The need for Task Expertise - or not

○ The need for Facilitative Expertise - or not

The need for Task Expertise is defined as the knowledge that a Mentor may have specifically related to the occupational activities of a Mentee.

The need for Facilitative Expertise is the ability to engage with the Mentee using a variety of interpersonal techniques that stimulate reflection and opportunities for growth.

The following diagram illustrates the Four Mentoring Styles which are explored in more detail on the following pages.

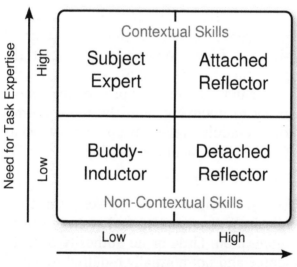

A Brief Overview of the Four Mentoring Styles

Mentoring Style 1: Buddy-Inductor

Some saw Mentoring primarily as a support and guidance for new members of staff; helping them settle in, become acquainted with their environment and the work processes that they will be using.

Some would say that this isn't Mentoring at all and dismiss it as what the Americans so neatly call 'Buddying'. But, if one thinks of the original source of the term, that of Odysseus' friend Mentor looking after the upbringing of Odysseus' son, then the 'adult-child' nature approximates more closely to buddying than the more normal 'adult-to-adult' relationship we associate with the term 'Mentoring' today.

Likely Mentor Background

Usually assigned to make someone, typically a new person, feel welcome to an organisation. Little or no authority over the Mentee and not normally required to advise on any issues other than the basic induction of someone into the workplace.

Value of the Relationship to the Mentee

- Up to speed quicker
- Remain enthusiastic and motivated
- Contribute new perspectives earlier

Value of the Relationship to the Mentor

- Feel valued for their experience
- Share knowledge and experiences
- Build valuable relationships

Value of the Relationship to the Organisation

- Individuals integrate into the organisation and reach a level of autonomy earlier
- Fresh perspectives provide valuable insights to organisations

Probable Relationship

- Team Colleague

Main Mentoring Activities

- Informs
- Warns
- Advises
- Guides

Mentee's need from the relationship

- Low task, Low reflective

The Different Mentoring Styles

Mentoring Style 2: Subject Expert

Some Mentees were not comfortable at all with any form of Mentor other than one whom they could go to with technical issues to resolve. Some individuals were very reluctant to engage in a relationship that was 'personal' in nature, but were very accepting of a relationship based on like minds solving work-related and usually technical conundrums.

Sometimes they felt their Mentor to be their manager, and sometimes they saw the Mentor as perhaps a peer with superior expertise in a given area. They very much esteemed such an individual and placed great value on the relationship they had.

Likely Mentor Background

Advises on issues that relate specifically to the Mentee's work. They provide instant help when the Mentee feels unsure and will show the Mentee new approaches. The Mentee will usually seek their help rather than the Mentor having responsibility for 'driving' the relationship.

Value of the Relationship to the Mentee

- Gains skills or knowledge specific to role
- Develops quicker with the support in specific subject areas

Value of the Relationship to the Mentor

- Feel valued for their knowledge
- Gains insights from a fresh perspective
- Able to practise the skills required in this area, e.g. providing constructive feedback

Value of the Relationship to the Organisation

- Individuals integrate into the organisation and reach a level of autonomy earlier
- Knowledge, experience and skills are shared throughout the organisation

Probable Relationship

- Manager or Section Head

Main Mentoring Activities

- Teaches
- Instructs
- Trains
- Feeds back

Mentee's need from the relationship

- High task, Low reflective

Mentoring Style 3: Attached Reflector

An Attached Reflector is more consistent with how managers often view a Mentor. They are often closely related in the hierarchy, perhaps a manager's manager or peer, and possess a considerable breadth of knowledge about the Mentee's working life. They differ from the Subject Expert in that they are only generally aware of the day-to-day work of their Mentee, but can bring complementary experience to any issue.

Another characteristic of this style of Mentoring is that they are, as one Mentee coined the phrase, a 'knowledgeable friend'. Their role is not to tell, but to ask the right questions and stimulate intellectual development on the part of the Mentee.

Likely Mentor Background

An authority on the Mentee's area of expertise, they are often valued as 'sounding boards' for the Mentee's ideas and aspirations about their work. Being separated from direct managerial responsibility for the Mentee, they see their role as one of a 'knowledgeable authority' to help them think more widely about what they do and how it fits into the 'bigger picture'.

Value of the Relationship to the Mentee

○ Gains a breadth and depth of thinking

○ Contextualises and shapes ideas and gains guidance in approach, tensions etc.,

Value of the Relationship to the Mentor

○ Provides an opportunity for practicing required skills e.g. coaching.

○ Contributies to an individual's growth which is rewarding in itself

○ Gains insights into their own thinking

Value of the Relationship to the Organisation

○ Encourages strong internal relationships and reflective practice

Probable Relationship

○ Mentee's Departmental Director

Main Mentoring Activities

○ Coaches

○ Listens

○ Advises

○ Guides

○ Feeds back

Mentee's need from the relationship

○ High task, High reflective

Mentoring Style 4: Detached Reflector

The Detached Mentor stimulates reflection and encourages the mental processes of the Mentee, but they differ in one key aspect; they have little or no knowledge of the Mentee's work, and this is their strength.

Sometimes, we found, a Mentor can be too close to a subject to be able to take 'the long view' of it. A Detached Reflector has no axe to grind, no agenda to pursue as they are not part of the general politics of the organisation. Such a distance has many advantages for the Mentee, particularly in offering the Mentee confidentiality.

It is more likely that this type of Mentor is sought independently by the Mentee and consequently valued more highly.

Likely Mentor Background

Respected for their thinking and the ability to deepen the thinking of others. They have no contact with any aspect of the Mentee's work, yet are valued for their ability to help the Mentee reflect on issues in the broadest possible sense. Being detached from the Mentee's workplace, they can let the Mentee look deeply at all aspects of their work with complete confidentiality.

Value of the Relationship to the Mentee

○ Gains an objective view in absolute confidence

Value of the Relationship to the Mentor

○ Gains an objective view without bias in absolute confidence

Value of the Relationship to the Organisation

○ Encourages individuals to network and build relationships that encourage a breadth of organisational thinking

Probable Relationship

○ Senior or highly respected figure from completely unrelated discipline

Main Mentoring Activities

○ Coaches
○ Listens
○ Advises
○ Guides
○ Feeds back

Mentee's need from the relationship

○ Low task, High reflective

Differentiating Between the Attached and Detached Reflectors

In the previous section concerning the Detached Reflector, I referred to their 'separateness' from the Mentee's working world. Let us explore this further by crystallising the distinct differences, and commonalities, that exist between the Attached and Detached Reflector.

Attached Reflectors are seen as often working within the Mentor's organisation and therefore regulated by the academic or business interests of that community. The Detached Reflector is not bound by these restrictions; because they pursue their activities external to the Mentee's workplace they can facilitate a Mentoring experience which enjoys far fewer constraints.

I've tried to capture this distinction in the following table.

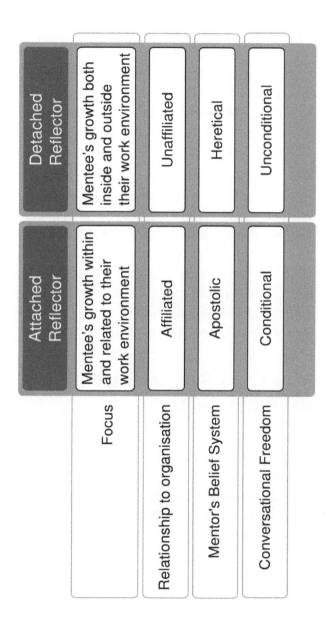

Focus	Attached Reflector — Mentee's growth within and related to their work environment	Detached Reflector — Mentee's growth both inside and outside their work environment
Relationship to organisation	Affiliated	Unaffiliated
Mentor's Belief System	Apostolic	Heretical
Conversational Freedom	Conditional	Unconditional

The Different Mentoring Styles

98

Earlier, you may have noticed that many of the activities and qualities of the Attached and Detached Reflector such as coaching, listening and challenging are the same. However, the arena within which these very activities are used might influence very different conversations.

For example, discontent with one's role and the way one perceives the political machinations within the organisation may not be appropriate for a conversation with an Attached Reflector. This is not to say that such conversations are not possible, but such 'treasonable talk' often proves more difficult when it is shared with someone who has a vested interest within that same organisation.

How Can I Be Sure That I Have the Right Mentor?

The following diagram illustrates the full span of Mentoring activity. Some Mentors may be able to satisfy the needs across the whole continuum whilst others may prefer that their activity occupies only a small area of the continuum.

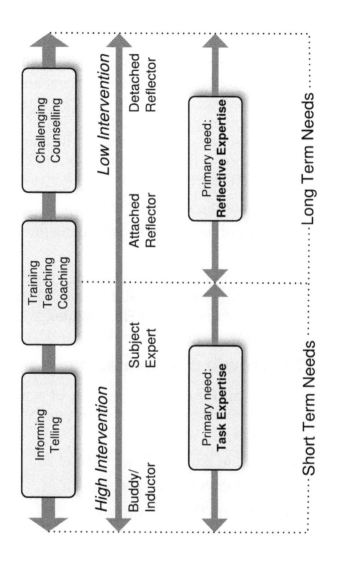

Self-knowledge

There might be an occasion where the self-knowledge of the Mentor is deficient and their statement of skills bears little resemblance to their actual skills. To help prevent this, you can find a role clarification questionnaire at the end of this book which helps the Mentor to identify:

o The Mentoring skills they have

o The Mentoring skills they are willing to use

It is also important that the Mentee's needs are assessed using a similar format. This should result in a 'Perfect Fit', resulting in a satisfying Mentoring relationship.

The Growth of a Mentee

Often the arrival of a new member of staff creates Mentoring needs over three separate dimensions:

o The need to acquire 'Environmental Fit'

o The need for 'Occupational Growth'

o The need for 'Personal Growth'

All fall under the influence of Mentoring but occur at staggered times during the first few weeks and months of the new arrival's appointment.

The first, Environmental Fit, could be looked upon as the essential foundation upon which the individual's career will be established. Environmental Fit covers the Mentoring activities that are normally associated with early induction: meeting the team and other key internal contacts, obtaining ID and Passwords, etc.

Occupational Growth is the increasing knowledge and understanding coupled with an improving ability to meet the ever-changing demands of the Mentee's new role. At first, the requirement of the Mentee is to 'grow into' the demands of the new position as they find it; they will then continue to push out their levels of understanding of their occupation.

Personal Growth is not synonymous with Occupational Growth. Rather it is the enhancement of an individual's generic skill sets and an increased capacity to apply a range of general strategies across the entire framework of their working life.

Personal growth satisfies the need to acquire generic
skills to increase individual learning effectiveness

Mentee's
Activities

Occupational Growth satisfies the need to discharge
the current demands of one's job more effectively

'Occupational Growth' is preoccupied with solutions that stabilise the individual's effectiveness in their current workplace; 'Personal Growth' is where the individual's activities and experiences come to be catalysts of personal learning which can be applied to a range of challenges and problems, many of which may sit outside their day-to-day work.

When the three dimensions are satisfied, one could state that the individual's progress within the new working environment is steadily moving through four stages of development, as shown in the following diagram.

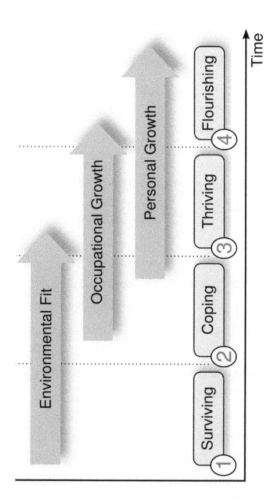

Why Some Mentee-Mentor Mismatches Can Occur

Early on in my research, I began to realise something that became almost axiomatic to the whole concept of Mentoring:

> The Mentor that a Mentee wants is not necessarily the Mentor that a Mentee needs

Not finding the right Mentor for a Mentee can be caused by a variety of factors which I have set out in a few scenarios below:

- The Mentee chooses a Mentor based on liking rather than developmental value
- The manager chooses a Mentor they know without consulting, and exploring the needs of, the Mentee
- The needs of the Mentee were not properly explored at the initial meeting
- The manager chooses someone with whom they enjoyed a close relationship in order to maintain control of the situation
- A Mentor is assigned who knows the Mentee personally, perhaps from a previous organisation

Hence the reason why I eventually entitled the project 'The Fit Mentor'; deciding on the most appropriate Mentor takes much more than the casual assignment of an individual without proper thought or discussion.

This is why the need for the manager to sit down and have an open, transparent conversation is absolutely paramount to the relationship's eventual success.

Practical Considerations for Mentoring

"The state of your life is nothing more than a reflection of your state of mind."

Dr. Wayne W. Dyer

Avoid tables where possible and arrange chairs in a non-confrontational layout

Ensure that heating and ventilation are acceptable to both parties

Make sure that mobile phones are turned off and limit interruptions

Private spaces, not crowded ones, are the most appropriate for Mentoring to be effective

Agree how often you want to meet and whether you wish to formally monitor your meetings or not

Different Strokes for Different Folks

One of the Mentors I met during my research told me of an instance when they conducted an initial Mentoring session on a golf course! The Mentee liked golf, as did the Mentor, and the first session, conducted over 18 holes, was an ideal icebreaker for both. It was the only session the Mentor conducted on the golf course with that individual, the organisation's offices being host to the subsequent sessions, but the manoeuvre had served its purpose: relaxing both the Mentee and Mentor and helping to cement a relationship built initially on a common interest.

Of course I'm not recommending that all relationships are kick-started in this way, but the general principle holds true that a little forethought can make a large contribution to the relationship's eventual success.

Furniture

Mentees are much more open when their physical needs are not distracting them, so a degree of thought needs to be given to some basic considerations.

If the session is to be for a reasonable period then comfortable chairs are a must. The arrangement of the chairs can also be significant. Arranging the chairs at an angle of 90 degrees avoids the 'confrontational' feel some people experience with chairs placed opposite each other. Such an arrangement also allows less confident individuals more opportunity for breaking eye contact.

Tables can be intrusive. If the only room you are able to meet in has a table then arrange the chairs around one corner; whatever you do, don't place the table between you and the other party.

Small details can often be overlooked. Will the sun shine brightly through a certain window? Is an open window causing a draught behind one person's chair? Is the chair too comfortable? Does one individual suffer from a bad back that might be exacerbated by a comfortably upholstered chair?

Lastly, the proximity of individuals to each other can be difficult for some to get right. Too far and the Mentee might find that the physical distance represents a corresponding coldness in the Mentor's manner. Too close and different signals might be sent!

Heating and Ventilation

Furniture is usually easy to get right; heating and ventilation that are comfortable for both can often prove another matter. Some people love the heat and hate fresh air; others become distracted if there is no fresh air and wilt under any source of direct heat.

Certain meeting spaces 'heat up' over the course of a Mentoring session, or there might be air conditioning that is controlled at a remote point in the building. A more reticent person might not say anything, but the discomfort might impair their ability to gain as much as they hope from the session.

It is usually the responsibility of Mentors to make the most appropriate arrangements; it is a selfish Mentor that automatically assumes that, if they are comfortable, then so is their Mentee.

Phone calls and Interruptions

Often, Mentoring can touch upon some profound areas of discussion. It only takes a knock at the door or the melody of a mobile phone for that moment to be lost, sometimes never to return. Even a detailed instruction from a Mentor can go off the rails when interrupted by something unforeseen.

There are, unfortunately, going to be occasions when an interruption is necessary, although with a little preparation, most potential distractions can be easily avoided. To do so sends a strong signal to the Mentee that the relationship is important to the Mentor too.

The whole purpose of Mentoring is to afford someone privileged access to another person's time. That principle is soon lost when it becomes apparent that such time is also equally accessed by other priorities.

One last point: the ubiquity of mobile phones has reached epidemic proportions, with many resting their phone by them so that they can 'take that important call'. Usually the call isn't very important at all, but this won't matter, because, whatever the nature of the call and however petty it might turn out to be, the conversation will have been interrupted.

The rule has to be that mobile phones are switched off. If you are expecting an important call, then see if this can be diverted to another person who can interrupt you when, and if, the call comes through. Once this has been dealt with, you are then able to continue with the rest of the session free of any further interruptions.

Public Areas

There are some who view a location like a bar or restaurant as a suitable place to hold a Mentoring session. My contention would be that it may be suitable for an initial rapport building session, but it may not prove to be a suitable atmosphere for any remaining Mentoring meetings.

Crowded spaces are distracting; even though the atmosphere might be lively and convivial, it is not conducive to reflection and, for those who seek Mentoring to provide an opportunity to consider their work in a profound way, will work against the very mental and interpersonal processes that make this successful.

Punctuality and Timing

In the section headed 'The Boundaries of Mentoring' we established that boundaries of time must be clearly agreed between both parties. Misuse of that time can be overlooked by some involved in Mentoring and this may lead to dissatisfaction about the effectiveness of the sessions.

The Mentor and Mentee must keep rigorously to the times agreed for the sessions. Such observance of time shows to each party that both invest a good degree of importance in the sessions. A tardy Mentee sends signals to the Mentor that they have little regard for the Mentor's time. A Mentor who shows equal disregard for punctuality sends the same signals to the Mentee.

Likewise, if one adopts the principle expounded in Parkinson's Law that "All meetings last as long as the time initially set aside for it" then it can be seen that, of equal importance, there is a need to agree a finishing time, and keep to it.

As pointed out in the section on boundaries, time is precious, and a desire to keep all meetings within their allotted time will be favourably received by all.

Refreshments

Refreshments are a basic courtesy in meetings; although many are careful to provide tea and coffee, perhaps the most welcome refreshment made available to both Mentor and Mentee is water. Research shows that it greatly assists mental concentration and, moreover, is universally appreciated; tea and coffee don't always have the same level of acceptability.

Regularity

My research indicated that both Mentors and Mentees have their own ideas about how often, and for how long, they should meet. As stated elsewhere, this is a subject for both parties to agree on at the outset. Do they envisage Mentoring being a regular occurrence, or do they anticipate a more informal basis driven by the Mentee's need to seek the advice or counsel of the Mentor?

Different Mentoring relationships call for different levels of support and contact; only by establishing a clear concord at the beginning will the regularity of the meetings work for the benefit of both parties.

Monitoring Progress

Some Mentors and Mentees have a strong desire to capture the outcomes of meetings, even using these as an 'aide-memoire' for use in subsequent meetings. Some Mentors and Mentees recoil from the very thought of formally recording the sum of their meetings.

As in so many areas covered already, what both parties feel works best will work best for them. If both Mentor and Mentee feel that the relationship is producing results then that may well be deemed sufficient as far as formalising the relationship is concerned.

Others may well think differently, and prefer to log the progress and outcomes of meetings in a more formalised, structured manner. Again, it is a matter for the discussions that precede the drawing up of the Mentoring contract.

Recommended Reading

The following books are all excellent recommendations for deepening your understanding of the skills, techniques, knowledge and philosophy that surround the fascinating area of Mentoring.

Everyone Needs a Mentor: Fostering Talent in Your Organisation, Clutterbuck, David, CIPD, 2004

Coaching for Performance, Whitmore, John, Nicholas Brealey Publishing, 2002

The Communication Catalyst, Connolly, Mickey and Rianoshek, Richard, Kaplan Publishing, 2002

The 7 Habits of Highly Effective People: Powerful Lessons in Personal Change, Covey, Stephen R, Simon and Schuster, 2004

The Luck Factor: The Scientific Study of the Lucky Mind, Wiseman, Richard, Arrow Books Ltd, 2004

Assertiveness at Work, Back, Ken and Back, Kate, McGraw Hill, 1999

Man's Search For Meaning: The classic tribute to hope from the Holocaust, Frankl, Viktor E, Rider; New edition (6 May 2004)

About the Author

Michael Heath is Managing Director of Michael Heath Consulting, a Learning and Development Consultancy established in the United Kingdom in 1999, providing leadership and employee workshops over a broad range of skill areas.

Drawing upon nearly 20 years' experience of working with an impressive portfolio of international organisations, he offers a wealth of practical knowledge and insights to address the challenges Mentors face.

If you would like to contact the author...

o About this book

o To present at your conference

o To facilitate a training programme for your organisation

o To receive the author's occasional newsletters

...then simply contact him at:

michael@mhconsult.com

The website for Michael Heath Consulting can be found here:

www.mhconsult.com

Acknowledgements

Much of this book would not have been possible without the invaluable input, encouragement and expertise of the following people:

Dr David Wilkinson

Ruth Altman

Sue Henshaw

Richard Butler

Professor David Clutterbuck's introduction sums up the essence of my work very well, and I am grateful to him for his contribution to my book, and of course to the field of mentoring, without which this book might not have been written.

I would also like to thank the Learning and Development Department at Cranfield University for facilitating much of the early research I undertook into Mentoring.

Role Clarification
Questionnaires

Mentor Questionnaire

This questionnaire will help you establish the type of Mentor you are prepared to be to your Mentee.

Look carefully at each statement and decide whether or not you would be prepared to offer this activity as part of your Mentoring role. If you do see it as something you would like to offer to your Mentee then put a tick in the adjacent box; if you do not see this as part of your Mentoring role then leave it blank.

As a Mentor, I am prepared to...

1. Advise on occupational best practice ☐

2. Help 'ease' the new Recruit into the ☐
   organisation

3. Encourage greater personal ☐
   awareness rather than achievement
   of immediate tasks

4. Knowledgeably challenge work- ☐
   related assumptions

As a Mentor, I am prepared to...

5. Encourage thinking towards the ☐
   much longer term

6. Guide the Mentee to complete a task ☐
   or undertake an assignment

7. Make sure that the Mentee is fully ☐
   employed in their daily work

8. Introduce the new recruit to working ☐
   colleagues and key contacts within
   the organisation

9. Explain the rules and regulations of ☐
   the work, especially related to basic
   employment entitlements

10. As a more experienced team ☐
    member, share my immediate
    experience with the Mentee

11. Play 'Devil's Advocate' about any ☐
    issues

As a Mentor, I am prepared to...

12. Find out information to help the □
individual with their work

13. Admit to no knowledge of a work □
subject but can 'trade ideas'

14. Take interest in broader □
development issues, not just short-
term needs

15. Help the individual put their work □
into a wider departmental context

16. Bring 'complementary experience' □
to the relationship

17. Make sure that the individual is □
competent

18. Draw out solutions to work placed □
problems

19. Focus on generic development □
rather than workplace growth

As a Mentor, I am prepared to...

20. Give work-related feedback ☐

21. Create ways for the Mentee to assess their working knowledge ☐

22. Be an operational support to the individual ☐

23. Advise and counsel on issues concerned with career change ☐

24. Consistently withhold personal opinions and judgement ☐

25. Explain the 'unwritten laws' of working within the organisation ☐

26. Withhold own opinions when helping the Mentee arrive at their own solutions to workplace issues ☐

27. Support the Mentee even if I have no real understanding of their work ☐

As a Mentor, I am prepared to...

28. Talk the new recruit through all of ☐
the Health and Safety issues
connected with their work

29. Having 'been on the journey', ask ☐
questions to help the Mentee
consider broader career options

30. Take the new recruit on a tour of ☐
the site

31. Draw on my expertise in the field ☐
without bias

32. Link personal growth to different ☐
workplace activities

33. Introduce personal contacts ☐
through peer networking

34. Encourage the individual to 'think ☐
outside the box'

As a Mentor, I am prepared to…

35. Arrange for all necessary personal ☐
    and IT security requirements (ID
    Card, Passwords, etc.) and ensure
    that they are working

36. Take the individual through the ☐
    different basic administrative
    processes and procedures necessary
    to carry out their work

37. Indicate the most effective books ☐
    and texts to support on-the-job
    work performance

38. Point the individual in the right ☐
    direction with their work

39. Facilitate discussions that help ☐
    identify detailed improvements to
    working practices

40. Acquaint the individual with the ☐
    'politics' within the organisation to
    help them settle in

Scoring

Score one point for each item you have ticked, with zero points for items you have left blank. Simply indicate on the list below which items were ticked.

Buddy-Inductor	Subject Expert	Attached Reflector	Detached Reflector
2	1	4	3
8	6	15	5
9	7	16	11
10	12	18	13
25	17	21	14
28	20	26	19
30	22	29	23
35	33	31	24
36	37	32	27
40	38	39	34
Totals			

The Fit Mentor

Once you have added up your totals look at the column with the highest score. The column with the highest score indicates the Mentoring style you are most naturally able to undertake in any Mentoring relationship.

If you find that you have two columns with equally high scores, then you have two Mentoring styles to move between.

The Mentee you would benefit the most is one who also seeks these skills in a Mentor.

Plot your scores on the chart below.

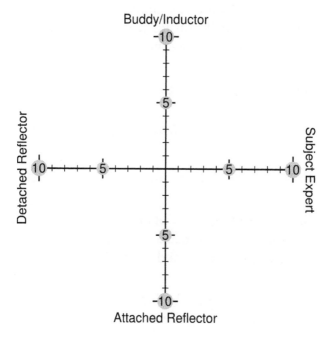

Mentee Questionnaire

This questionnaire will help you establish the most suitable Mentor for you. Achieving the right Mentor 'fit' will help ensure that your needs from the Mentoring relationship are met.

Look carefully at each statement and decide whether or not you view the activity as something you would expect your Mentor to do for you as part of their role. If you do see it as something you would expect your Mentor to do for you then put a tick in the adjacent box; if you do not see this as part of your Mentor's role then leave it blank.

I expect my Mentor to...

1. Advise on occupational best practice ☐

2. Help 'ease' me into the organisation ☐

3. Encourage greater personal ☐
    awareness in me rather than point
    me towards immediate tasks

4. Knowledgeably challenge my work- ☐
    related assumptions

I expect my Mentor to...

5. Encourage my thinking towards the ☐
   much longer term

6. Guide me how to complete a task or ☐
   undertake an assignment

7. Make sure that I am fully employed ☐
   in my day-to-day work

8. Introduce me to working colleagues ☐
   and key contacts within the
   organisation

9. Explain the rules and regulations of ☐
   my work, especially related to my
   basic employment entitlements

10. As a more experienced team ☐
    member, share their immediate
    experience with me

11. Play 'Devil's Advocate' ☐

12. Find out information to help me ☐
    with my work

I expect my Mentor to...

13. Have no knowledge of a work- ☐
    related subject but be someone
    who can 'trade ideas' with me

14. Take interest in my broad ☐
    development issues, not short-term
    needs

15. Help me put my work into a wider ☐
    departmental context

16. Bring 'complementary experience' ☐
    to our relationship

17. Make sure that I am competent ☐

18. Draw out solutions to work placed ☐
    problems

19. Focus on generic development ☐
    issues rather than workplace
    growth

20. Give work-related feedback ☐

I expect my Mentor to...

21. Create opportunities for me to ☐
    assess my working knowledge

22. Be an operational support to me ☐

23. Advise and counsel on issues ☐
    concerned with career change

24. Consistently withhold personal ☐
    opinions and judgement and let me
    arrive at my own solutions

25. Explain the 'unwritten laws' of ☐
    working within my organisation

26. Withhold their own opinions when ☐
    helping me arrive at my own
    solutions to workplace issues

27. Support me even if they have no ☐
    real understanding of my work

28. Talk me through all of the Health ☐
    and Safety issues connected with
    my work

I expect my Mentor to...

29. Because they've 'been on the ☐
    journey', ask questions to help me
    consider my broader career options

30. Take me on a tour of the site ☐

31. Draw on their expertise in the field ☐
    without bias

32. Link my personal growth to ☐
    different workplace activities

33. Introduce personal contacts ☐
    through peer networking

34. Encourage me to 'think outside the ☐
    box'

35. Arrange for all personal and IT ☐
    security requirements (ID Card,
    Passwords, etc.) and ensure that
    they are working

I expect my Mentor to...

36. Take me through basic
    administrative processes and
    procedures necessary for my work ☐

37. Indicate the most effective books
    and texts to support my on-the-job
    work performance ☐

38. Point me in the right direction with ☐
    my work

39. Facilitate discussions that help me ☐
    identify detailed improvements to
    working practices

40. Acquaint me with the detailed ☐
    'politics' existing within the
    organisation to help me settle in

Scoring

Score one point for each item you have ticked, with zero points for items you have left blank. Simply indicate on the list below which items were ticked.

	2	1	4	3
	8	6	15	5
	9	7	16	11
	10	12	18	13
	25	17	21	14
	28	20	26	19
	30	22	29	23
	35	33	31	24
	36	37	32	27
	40	38	39	34
Totals				
	Buddy-Inductor	Subject Expert	Attached Reflector	Detached Reflector

Once you have added up your totals look at the column with the highest score. The column with the highest score indicates the Mentoring style you are most naturally likely to benefit from in any Mentoring relationship.

If you find that you have two columns with equally high scores, then you have two Mentoring styles that you can easily choose between.

Plot your scores on the chart below.

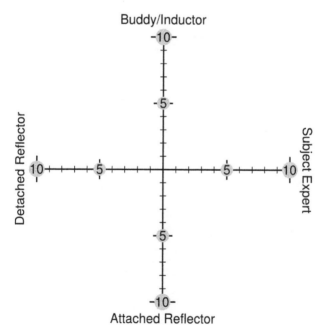

Mentoring Evaluation Questionnaires

Mentor Questionnaire

Mentor Name:

Mentor Organisation:

Mentee Name:

Mentoring Start Date:

Questionnaire Completion Date:

It is important to get your views on the Mentoring relationship you are engaged in. Think carefully about the questions and give your honest answers. Your views will help us ensure that any future Mentoring relationships are beneficial and worthwhile. Any additional comments you wish to make will be very helpful.

1. As a Mentor, what were the original objectives you wanted to achieve through the Mentoring relationship?

2. How fully were your objectives met?

3. What other principal areas that weren't in your original objectives have you also made progress on?

4. In which ways have you most benefited from the Mentoring relationship?

5. What worked well in your Mentoring relationship?

6. What worked less well or could have been improved?

7. How do you believe your Mentee has translated their Mentoring experience back into their workplace?

My Mentee...

8. ...was approachable and easy to talk to

9. ...met with me regularly

10. ...met with me in a suitable environment for the Mentoring sessions

11. ...was facilitated and encouraged by me to think rather than just let me do the thinking for them

12. ...took part in the meetings with integrity and the appropriate level of confidentiality

13. ...appeared comfortable with my Mentoring style

14. ...agreed specific goals that they could work on after each Mentoring session

15. What recommendations would you make to other Mentor–Mentee pairs?

16. What general comments do you have about the Mentoring Scheme?

This questionnaire can be downloaded from the author's website: www.mhconsult.com

Mentee Questionnaire

Mentee Name:

Mentor Name:

Mentor Organisation:

Mentoring Start Date:

Questionnaire Completion Date:

It is important to get your views on the Mentoring relationship you are engaged in. Think carefully about the questions and give your honest answers. Your views will help us ensure that any future Mentoring relationships are beneficial and worthwhile. Any additional comments you wish to make will be very helpful.

1. What were the original objectives you wanted to achieve through the Mentoring relationship?

2. How fully were your Mentoring objectives met?

3. What other principal areas that weren't in your original objectives have you also made progress on?

4. In which ways have you most benefited from the Mentoring relationship?

5. What worked well in your Mentoring relationship?

6. What worked less well or could have been improved?

7. How have you translated the Mentoring experience back into your workplace?

My Mentor...

8. ...was approachable and easy to talk to

9. ...met with me regularly

10. ...met with me in a suitable environment for the Mentoring sessions

11. ...facilitated and encouraged my thinking rather than just did all the thinking for me

12. ...conducted the meetings with integrity and the appropriate level of confidentiality

13. ...used a Mentoring style that I was comfortable with

14. ...agreed specific goals that I could work on after each Mentoring session

15. What recommendations would you make to other Mentor–Mentee pairs?

16. What general comments do you have about the Mentoring Scheme?

This questionnaire can be downloaded from the author's website: www.mhconsult.com

Lightning Source UK Ltd.
Milton Keynes UK
UKHW010424210819
348299UK00003B/988/P